T0333289

LAND ROVER

GRIPPING PHOTOS OF THE 4x4 PIONEER

GILES CHAPMAN

The History Press

First published 2020
Reprinted 2021, 2023

The History Press
97 St George's Place,
Cheltenham GL50 3QB
www.thehistorypress.co.uk

British Library Cataloguing in Publication Data.
A catalogue record for this book is available from the British Library.

ISBN 978 0 7509 9319 7

Typesetting and origination by The History Press
Printed in India by Thomson Press

INTRODUCTION

There is now, as you read this, a brand new Land Rover Defender. There needs to be. The original came to the end of the line in 2016, before the word 'Brexit' had ever been uttered, and for Land Rover diehards its departure left a gaping hole not just in the supporting wall of the British motor industry but in the fabric of the country itself. It was like someone had banned cricket from the village green, or decreed Christmas lunch was henceforth to be strictly vegan. The original Land Rover, stretching unbroken along a muddy timeline from 1948 to 2016, was a proper institution.

The main reason we had to wave the four-wheel-drive pioneer goodbye was because, in today's world, the final Land Rover Defender was at the absolute limits of its ability to comply with regulations governing the construction of, and emissions from, new vehicles. Even in 2006, the rules had started to impinge on it, when the side-facing seats in the back of station wagons were deemed unsafe. It didn't have any crumple zones and there were never any airbags. The Land Rover Defender hails from a far-back time when those things hadn't even been imagined.

The idea for the Land Rover arose on a farm in north Wales. There, in 1947, one of the directors of Rover, maker of quality cars for the affluent middle classes, was having problems with a battered Second World War Jeep that he used for odd jobs. When it worked, its four-wheel drive and light controls made it the best thing in the world for belting across fields to reach stricken livestock or broken fences. When it broke, though, Maurice Wilks was forced to drag its sorry carcass back to the Rover factory in Solihull, near Birmingham, for repairs. Being a bit of old war surplus in an austere and penniless Britain, getting hold of spare parts was impossible.

Another thing that Rover was having trouble getting its hands on was the steel required to start making the saloon cars beloved of doctors and solicitors in Britain's leafy suburbs. Surrounded by problems, though, Wilks suddenly had a brainwave. Could Rover get through the tough times by making its own version of the Jeep, only not tilted at armies but at landowners and farmers? If they could build it from something other than steel then perhaps it would work. Just as his Jeep was a relic of the recent conflict, so there was quite a lot of unused aircraft-grade aluminium sheet kicking around. And so it was that Wilks and Rover's engineers formulated their plans for a 'Land Rover'.

Their starting point, logically enough, was a Jeep chassis and axles, but the 1.4-litre, four-cylinder engine was from a Rover car, and the single seat was in the middle of the car in the style of the hybrid tractor/pick-up that Wilks envisioned.

A pretty sophisticated four-wheel-drive system was devised with driveshafts to the front and back and power transmitted through a specially designed transfer case. The four-wheel drive was permanent, and used a freewheel device on the front driveshaft to allow for front and rear wheels revolving at slightly different speeds.

There was a lot of scepticism inside Rover about the venture, but the prototype was built in just a few weeks and everyone who drove it was immediately impressed by its potential. Its tenacious grip and ability to claw its way up steep and slippery inclines was a revelation. The board was persuaded to approve it and, because it was viewed as a stopgap product that could be built cheaply using jigs and hand tools, it wasn't going to break the bank.

Wilks saw it not just as a go-anywhere vehicle but a do-anything vehicle. He insisted there should be 'power take-off' points front, middle and rear. That way, the vehicle could be driven somewhere remote but still be used as a power source to animate anything from a circular saw to welding gear. All sound, ultra-practical thinking.

Rover soon ditched the central seat for traditional right- or left-hand drive with two more small passenger seats alongside. They wanted solutions and not problems, after all, and now that production was going ahead a more powerful 1.6-litre Rover engine was fitted, a strong chassis with tough leaf springs was designed, and the simple aluminium body became more boxy and flat-planed in a quest to make it as cheap and easy to manufacture as possible. From being a crude, Rover-powered Jeep, the Land Rover was its own man and ready to meet the public for the first time at the Amsterdam Motor Show in April 1948.

It made a huge impact and the production line cranked into life four months later making ten Land Rovers a day; it went on sale at £540. By then a true appreciation of the Land Rover's potential had formed and a few orders had trickled in. Not bad for a vehicle that hadn't even existed two years earlier but it all still felt like a big, risky step into the dark.

Early owners, however, were astonished at how the Land Rover could bounce across rutted fields and charge up hills with gusto, and that its excellent wheel articulation and approach/departure angles of 45/35 degrees meant it could pick its way over just about anything. It wasn't fast but there was plenty of torque for what really mattered – pulling power.

Buyers were immediately won over by this no-frills workhorse with panels that couldn't rust. To own one was never to be without one again, and the word soon spread. Rover hoped to shift 5,000 annually but in its first financial year sold 8,000. In 1949–50, sales doubled and the company was then selling two Land Rovers for every one Rover car. Quite unexpectedly, the tail was now wagging the dog, and it wasn't just the agricultural world that had woken up to the Land Rover's tactical advantages. Police forces, electricity boards, forest rangers, building contractors and adventurers all ordered them and, from 1950, so did the British Army.

The booming popularity brought plenty of feedback and Rover responded by starting a rolling programme of improvements. The first, and most significant, came in 1950, when the freewheel was dropped. In order to properly co-ordinate the front and rear wheels, four-wheel drive was now selectable thanks to a simple but ingenious dogleg clutch mechanism. In high-ratio range for road use, the Land Rover could be driven in two- or four-wheel drive, but four-wheel drive now engaged automatically when the low range was chosen.

By the end of 1951 the engine had expanded in size to a 2-litre, which boosted torque for low-speed, heavyweight duties. This was, it was understood, mostly a commercial vehicle, and demands for more cargo space saw the wheelbase increase from 80in (identical to the old Willys Jeep) to 86in in 1953, when an even longer 107in wheelbase joined it. Just one year later sales hit 100,000, and no one was more surprised than Maurice Wilks that Rover's little sideline had now become its most crucial asset.

In 1956, wheelbases were up again to 88 and 109in as the engine bay was modified to take Land Rover's first diesel engine, extending fuel consumption from 22 to 35mpg. Land Rovers were becoming a common sight all over the world – with some 70 per cent exported – and the fact that there was nothing else like it on sale threw up a conundrum for the BBC. If a Land Rover was reported on radio or television on a battlefield or royal parade, reporters were not allowed to use the brand name, and the BBC had to coin the term 'field car' to dodge the issue.

Almost 200,000 Land Rovers had been built by 1958, when the arrival of the Series II forever rendered the earlier model the mightily revered Series I. Roomier and more substantial bodies and bigger engines culminated in the Series IIA of 1961. Annual output peaked at 56,564 in 1971, which included many kits of parts assembled into Land Rovers in far-flung corners of the globe. By the time the Series III model range took its bow that year the Land Rover operation found itself part of the ill-starred British Leyland organisation. The tough-as-old-boots, four-wheel-drive pick-ups, station wagons and vans could be profitably adapted in myriad ways for any number of special purposes, and the Range Rover sister marque had broken totally new ground in offering a luxurious off-roader with a coil-sprung chassis that made it as smooth to drive on tarmac as it was relentless in the rough. Little wonder that Land Rover Ltd became a separate entity in 1978, with a £200 million war chest to spend on new models. While most of the focus was on improving the Range Rover, Series III Land Rovers received a powerful V8 engine option.

The most fundamental change in the Land Rover's long and illustrious career, though, occurred in 1983. As sales were growing of Toyota's Hilux and other Japanese-made four-wheel-drive pick-ups, the old-fashioned leaf springs in the Land Rover, the components that by then severely hampered its on-road appeal due to the bumpy and uncompromising ride quality, just had to go. So in came a new Range Rover-style chassis frame complete with heavy-duty coil-spring suspension all round. Now Land Rovers were at least tolerable on long road trips, especially when towing horseboxes or vehicle trailers. Slight wheelbase increases to 90 and 110in were accompanied by a switch to full-time four-wheel drive as the Range Rover's five-speed gearbox was also standardised. There were a few more concessions to the modern motoring world too, such as wind-down windows instead of sliding ones, while a wider track improved roadholding.

These new Land Rovers were, without doubt, the most capable four-wheel-drive vehicles for serious work on all kinds of demanding terrain. With their separate chassis frames and modular construction, they were also still the most readily adaptable of vehicles, able to be specified and custom-built any which way for roles from the battlefield to the building site. Suddenly, though, there were a lot of other options around as more car-like and civilised off-roaders arrived from Japan to tempt buyers away from the hardcore Land Rover. It no longer had to try and be all things to all men; after the Land Rover Discovery sport-utility vehicle (SUV) arrived in 1989, the 90 and 110 were rebranded as the Defender and began to have the specialised market for a no-compromise off-roader all to themselves.

Still, the traditional Landies were labouring under a burden that was impossible to alter. The stout separate chassis, being the main load-bearing component, could not be anything other than heavy and substantial; there were limits to how fuel efficient a Defender could be as a result, and not much could be done to improve its active or passive safety, all of which were matters of pressing legislative importance in the 1990s and 2000s. Something like the 1984 Jeep Cherokee offered consumers the lofty driving position and excellent off-road performance they yearned for, but featured car-like road manners and could be fitted with every modern safety feature. The Defender, frankly, was a cumbersome 1960s lorry by comparison even if, in the final reckoning, it was still the most able vehicle in the severest off-road conditions.

In 1990, the staple Land Rover gained its own 'textual' model name for the first time: Defender. Simultaneously, a turbodiesel engine was offered. Four years after that the venerable V8 power unit was axed, in the UK at least, and in another four years' time the staple engine became a brand new, and far more responsive, five-cylinder turbodiesel, the Td5, with a computer-controlled electronic fuel-injection system and a centrifugal oil filter to extend service intervals.

In the 1990s and 2000s, the Land Rover organisation changed hands like a country girl at a barn dance, being owned (in chronological order) by British Aerospace, BMW, Ford and finally India's Tata, which merged it with Jaguar to form by far the biggest British-based car-making group. Throughout all of the head office changes, though, the Land Rover Defender production line plodded on unchanged. Only in 2006 did the vehicles gain a raft of improvements to keep them just about abreast of modern standards. They included a totally redesigned dashboard (more user-friendly but meaning the swivelling air vents under the windscreen had to be sealed up for good), a new heating and ventilation system, a less-polluting 2.4-litre turbodiesel engine specially adapted from the Ford Transit for off-road use, a six-speed gearbox and a more refined, quieter transfer box. The bonnet sprouted a prominent bulge so the new engine could be positioned to allow deformable space in the event of a pedestrian impact.

It was all worthwhile stuff, because Land Rover was still selling 20,000 to 25,000 Defenders every year. The majority, without doubt, were gainfully employed in no-nonsense tasks on farms, with rescue services, in industry and in countless other roles. Yet the Defender's living-legend status still saw plenty of private motorists choosing it as an everyday car that was, now, quite unlike anything else on sale.

In off-road forays, naturally, it was completely at home wading through water or marshland, or else bouncing its way over shingle or rocky outcrops. On the highway it was nothing like as comfortable or responsive as a 'normal' car, but life in the slow lane was no deterrent to its most ardent fans. Not just that but the Defender's absolute form-following-function profile gave it a time-honoured credibility that marked its owners out as lovers of true originals.

Some of all this has inspired this book. If you have owned or driven one of these awe-inspiring British vehicles then you'll fully recognise them in all the various situations in which they are illustrated. But if you simply love the idea of traditional Land Rovers then maybe the content – including many previously unpublished photos, and others that fully capture the essence of the marque – will inspire you to get one of your own … and head for the hills with a big grin and a firm grasp on the steering wheel.

A true hero of the Second World War, the all-wheel drive Willys Jeep (the name fuses the capital letters and pronunciation of General Purpose) proved its worth countless times as a battlefield taxi, troop carrier and reconnaissance vehicle. You'd be amazed at how easy and pleasant it is to drive even today. Here was the world's first lightweight go-anywhere vehicle, and far too sound an idea to be left behind to history.

OPPOSITE: In its CJ (for Civilian Jeep) guise the compact warhorse was repurposed for the rigours of life in American agriculture and industry. They called it the 'Universal' but in truth most sales were confined to the US. Other countries either took out licences to make them locally or came up with their own copies. You certainly couldn't buy one in Britain, nor anything remotely like it …

LAND ROVER

WHEN THE GOING IS TOUGH, when you have a heavy load to pull, the Universal "Jeep's" 4-wheel drive puts amazing tractive power at your command. That's why the "Jeep" can haul supplies through mud and snow . . . take workers across roadless countrysides . . . pull almost any farm implement. The front drive-axle of the "Jeep" is a "business end" that broadens the utility of this versatile vehicle for industry and the farm.

THE 'JEEP' HAS TWO 'BUSINESS ENDS'

2 or 4 Wheel Drive, Plus Power Take-off, for Widest Utility

ON THE HIGHWAY and around town, you drop back to conventional 2-wheel drive to save on the economy of the world-famous Willys-Overland "Jeep" Engine. And if you have belt- or shaft-driven equipment to operate, the power take-off on the rear makes your "Jeep" a mobile power unit.

Your Willys-Overland dealer can show you why the Universal "Jeep," with its two business ends, can do more jobs for you at lower cost.

Willys-Overland Motors
TOLEDO, OHIO
MAKERS OF AMERICA'S MOST USEFUL VEHICLES

FOR ECONOMICAL POWER . . . FOR ALL-AROUND VERSATILITY

GET A 'Jeep'

GRIPPING PHOTOS OF THE 4X4 PIONEER

Maurice Wilks, chief
engineer of the Rover
Company, used a worn-out,
war-surplus Jeep on his farm in Anglesey.
When it went wrong, which was often, it was sent
to the company's workshops for surgery. It was 1947,
economically bleak, and Rover urgently needed a new project.
Suddenly the penny dropped: why not make something similar but
better? Maurice and his brother, Rover boss Spencer Wilks, are said to have
drawn their brainwave out on the Anglesey beach. It probably looked a bit like this.

LAND ROVER

The 'centre-steer' prototype is thought to be lost forever but is regarded as such a unicorn among today's Land Rover enthusiasts that this recreation was built to show younger generations where the vehicle came from.

OPPOSITE TOP: By September 1947, the first prototype was coming together in Rover's Solihull engineering department. This is the earliest known picture. The team saved time by using an old Jeep chassis and axles as a starting point, then installed a Rover 10 engine and designed their own transfer case to distribute power to all four wheels.

OPPOSITE BOTTOM: Here is the original prototype undergoing the most literal of 'field tests', hitched up to a plough. The Wilks brothers saw their vehicle as a sort of hybrid tractor/pick-up, hence the single seat in the middle. It was intended as the most useful possible piece of agricultural equipment in any landowner's armoury.

GRIPPING PHOTOS OF THE 4X4 PIONEER

ABOVE: An essential part of any off-roader is its ability to stay upright on the rockiest of roads. Here's how they did the 'tilt test' at the factory at a time when digital measuring devices couldn't even be imagined.

LEFT: The Land Rover production line cranks into life in 1948. The ultra-simple body panels were mostly pressed by hand to cut down on tooling costs. In fact, the whole enterprise was done on a shoestring in those austerity times simply to keep Rover's factory busy until it could secure enough steel supplies to start making more cars.

LAND ROVER

A period advert for the early Land Rover got the message across in a beautifully simple way. It was first revealed to British farmers at the Bath & West agricultural show in summer 1948, and thousands made up their minds to get one.

NO ROAD
EXCEPT FOR LAND ROVER

The man in the blue anorak being driven is Arthur Goddard, the engineer put in charge of the Land Rover project. He came over from Australia in 2010 to be reunited here with the vehicle he built and one of its original test routes, through Packington Ford in Warwickshire.

OPPOSITE TOP: The Series 1 with its 80in wheelbase, showing the flimsy sidescreens that formed the upper parts of the doors, and the spare wheel bolted to the top of the bonnet.

OPPOSITE BOTTOM: With the spare wheel behind the seats, the windscreen could be folded flat, like a sports car.

GRIPPING PHOTOS OF THE 4X4 PIONEER

In 2016, Land Rover's Classic division restored twenty-five Series I vehicles to absolutely authentic original order, every bolt and rivet just as it left the factory. Here is the extremely basic driving environment presented in immaculate order.

LAND ROVER

A view over the driver's shoulder inside the detail-perfect 1948 Series I. If you've ever thought all these early Land Rovers seem to be in dark green, you're spot on; the paint, formerly used on Avro aircraft, was bought as a war-surplus job lot.

The hyphen quirk: it appeared as a zigzag on the Land Rover badge but has never been used anywhere else.

LAND ROVER

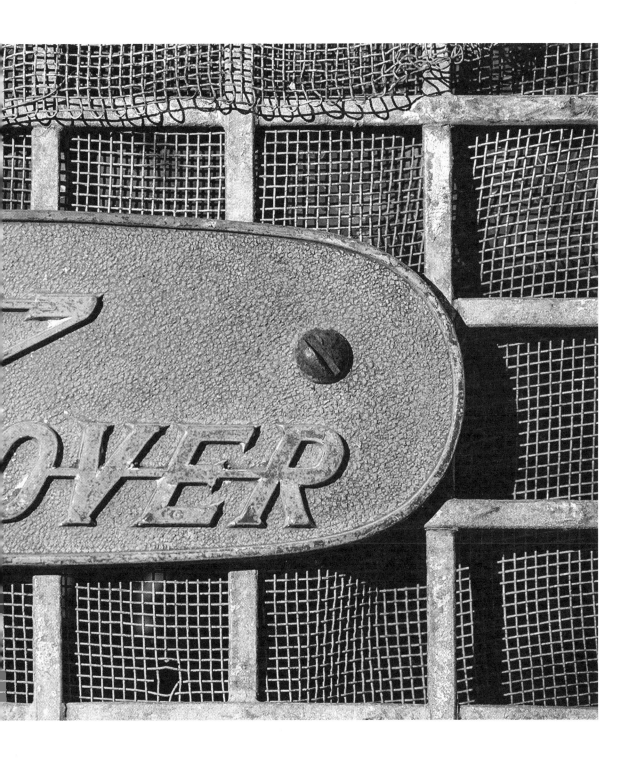

GRIPPING PHOTOS OF THE 4X4 PIONEER

The canvas tilt, with its pillbox gap for rear visibility, kept the rain out but rarely all the draughts, fitting like a tent over a simple tubular frame.

LAND ROVER

Avon Tyres made the special Trackgrip rubber fitted to the Series I. This painstakingly restored example is pluckily making its way over Land Rover's dedicated test circuit at Eastnor Castle near Ledbury, Herefordshire.

GRIPPING PHOTOS OF THE 4X4 PIONEER

Twenty-three-year-old racing driver Stuart Lewis-Evans unloading his Cooper 500 Formula 3 racing car at Crystal Palace race circuit in 1953. The Land Rover was more than robust enough to make a homespun transporter but must have been unnerving to drive with a whole car balanced precariously on its roof. Stuart's Formula 1 career was short, intense and tragic; he was killed in the 1958 Moroccan Grand Prix.

If you wanted a life-changing adventure, then a Land Rover would prove ideal. These are Canadians Bristol Foster and Robert Bateman arriving at the Rover factory in 1957 to collect theirs, fitted with an ambulance body, and about to embark on a 37,000-mile trip through nineteen countries across four continents. Their meandering route of more than fourteen months took them through the Belgian Congo, where thirty members of the Mbuti tribe hitched a ride, and in India they overturned the vehicle trying to avoid a cyclist.

LAND ROVER

Revelling in the rolling waves of the Cape Town coast, from the moving vantage point of a Land Rover Series I with a factory-supplied hardtop to keep the hot sun at bay.

GRIPPING PHOTOS OF THE 4X4 PIONEER

This is the actual Land Rover prototype that made its global debut at the Amsterdam Motor Show in April 1948. A priceless icon of the marque's rich heritage, it underwent a year-long restoration in 2018, a delicate task that sought to keep as much of the original patina and unique features – including a galvanised chassis and detachable rear tub – as possible.

LAND ROVER

At some time in its life, this long-suffering Land Rover was converted from its original left- to right-hand drive and somehow survived in the West Midlands despite being left to rot away in a back garden for twenty years.

As early as autumn 1948, Land Rover was considering a more civilised and comfortable off-roader, with this station wagon boasting a handsome coach-built body.

The bodywork was created by Tickford, the Newport Pagnell artisans forever associated with Aston Martin. It was a six-seater with leather upholstery that nevertheless proved rather too costly to be popular with buyers.

A neat touch on the Tickford station wagon, seen here in actual station collection duty, was the metal cover to shroud the spare wheel.

LAND ROVER

ABOVE: Four-wheel-drive grip and high ground clearance made the Land Rover a new hero for rescue services. These two have brought AA patrolmen to a heavily snowbound Highlands spot in the mid-1950s to dig out an Austin A40 Somerset for its stricken owner.

RIGHT: Essential reading material for all Series I owners, with a useful reminder on the cover to have an oil can handy in the workshop …

GRIPPING PHOTOS OF THE 4X4 PIONEER

So spotless you could eat your cheese and pickle sandwich off it. This studio shot of a well-known Series I lays bare the Land Rover's complete absence of frippery for all to see. Everything, from the single wing mirror to the simple mesh stone guard over the headlights and radiator is just sufficient to get the job done.

OPPOSITE: Taken, it is thought, on a British race circuit perimeter road in about 1964, where Dunlop promotion is heavily in evidence; Land Rovers such as this Series I were always great for rapid access across sprawling sites, and just about every other motorised duty.

GRIPPING PHOTOS OF THE 4X4 PIONEER

LAND ROVER

Photographer Sam Shaw took this informal image of his friend Marilyn Monroe in a Series I in 1957, on the Amagansett, Long Island, beach where she often went, ironically, to escape the limelight.

GRIPPING PHOTOS OF THE 4X4 PIONEER

Land Rover had a rethink on its station wagon and launched this new version in 1954, now with utterly functional, rectilinear bodywork produced at the factory. It featured the first of the leathercloth-type 'safari' roof coverings to keep the interior cool in summer and condensation-free in winter.

The narrow window panes in the roof edges first appeared here and would remain familiar in every station wagon to the end of the Defender's life sixty-two years later.

RIGHT: Designer Marcel Van Cleemput at Corgi Toys proved masterful in reducing the size of a Land Rover 107in pick-up to roughly 1:47 scale in 1957. Now prospective young owners could hold it in their hands first.

BELOW: The arrival of a longer, 107in wheelbase model in 1953 made the Land Rover ever more adaptable to unique iterations. This mechanical ensemble is a mobile machine for testing the quality of golf balls, harnessing the vehicle's rear power-take-off function to animate the machine that hurled the balls with realistic vigour.

GRIPPING PHOTOS OF THE 4X4 PIONEER

LAND ROVER

It really is curious that a mechanical device can look so at home in the rolling, natural contours of the British countryside, but this utterly delightful vehicle does just that. This is 'Huey', named for its registration number of HUE 166, which is the very first pre-production Land Rover Series I. It has been treasured and maintained in working order by the factory since the 1960s.

Sir Winston Churchill was presented with this Land Rover Series I on his 80th birthday on 30 November 1954, when he was still Prime Minister. He loved driving it around his 300-acre country estate at Chartwell, Kent, especially as it had a trunk in the back contained bricklaying tools for his favourite form of relaxation (no, really). It also had an extra-wide seat and a heated footwell specially for him. It was only taxed for road use in 1967, two years after Churchill's passing. In 2012, it sold at auction in a dilapidated state for £129,000.

OPPOSITE: Her Majesty the Queen and the Duke of Edinburgh find it easy to inspect the Royal Navy aircraft carrier HMS Albion aboard the warship's very own Series I Land Rover in 1957. The vessel, nicknamed the 'Old Grey Ghost of the Borneo Coast', was then ten years old.

Back to back across four decades: a fascinating contrast between the Series I 80in wheelbase on the left and its direct descendant, the 90in wheelbase 90 County station wagon, pictured in 1988.

Loaded up and headed overseas, this consignment of Land Rover Series IIs was but a tiny fraction of the thousands that were bought all over the world. Many more were exported as kits for local assembly everywhere from Iran to Cuba. Rover produced 110,000 Series IIs in just three years.

ABOVE: As seen all over the British countryside by the 1960s; a Land Rover Series II 88in pick-up with tilt and plenty of mud splashed along its flanks.

RIGHT: A decidedly rugged setting for the first of the new Series II models, with deeper body panels and more interior space. In this case the car actually photographed was the fifth prototype built.

GRIPPING PHOTOS OF THE 4X4 PIONEER

LAND ROVER

ABOVE: Ultimately, Campbell's record attempt at Utah failed when he crashed his Bluebird at 360mph, fracturing his skull and bursting an eardrum. But he tried again in 1964, here at Lake Eyre in Australia (a Land Rover just visible on the left), and became the fastest 'car' driver on earth at 403mph.

OPPOSITE TOP: When Donald Campbell decided to challenge the World Land Speed Record in 1960 with his Proteus-Bluebird CN7, Rover was eager to assist with all the Land Rover support vehicles he needed. Here Campbell gives a demo run in Britain beforehand, accompanied by a Series 1 107in pick-up.

OPPOSITE BOTTOM: Land Rovers helped out in all sorts or roles, as fire tenders and air compressor carriers, at the record attempt at the Bonneville Salt Flats in Utah, USA. There was obvious synergy because Rover had been experimenting with its own gas turbine 'jet' engines since the 1940s.

GRIPPING PHOTOS OF THE 4X4 PIONEER

The scene just before Britain's first purpose-built motorway, the M1, opened in 1959. The AA is ready for action with a spanking new fleet of Series II patrol vehicles with two-way radios, all ready for the new high-speed era. The four other patrol cars are Ford 100E Squire estates. There would be plenty to attend to: very few British cars were capable of 70mph cruising without overheating, and the lack of central reservation barriers meant continual accident carnage from head-on smashes.

With the growth of private car ownership in the 1950s and '60s, the AA's Land Rovers worked around the clock. Here an anxious motorist waits to find out if his Hillman Minx can be patched up to continue its journey, as the mechanic patrolman works his way through the toolbox in the back of his Series II.

LAND ROVER

The astonishing Roadless Traction Company Land Rover 109in pick-up conversion added gigantic tractor wheels and truck axles, with altered gearing and an increased front track to make the beast easily driveable in all conditions. It was a factory-approved conversion, of which nine were made.

The Roadless idea grew originally from Britain's Forestry Commission in 1959, which wanted something extra-capable to surmount deep ditches and small ravines, and to drive over large fallen trees. Little surprise it was nicknamed the 'Forest Rover'. Here an early prototype is being put through some gruelling testing.

'On safari' had meant riding out on horseback or lurking in claw-proof hides if you wanted to see Africa's most dramatic wildlife. Now, as hunting started to give way to conservation, Land Rovers such as this Series II station wagon were ideal as a mobile viewing gallery out in the bush.

So well suited were Land Rovers for official duties that the company made these two Series II 'Review' vehicles for Buckingham Palace in 1959. In addition to the lofty platform on which the Queen could slowly inspect her immaculate ranks of servicemen, they featured a special aluminium grille, chrome hubcaps and the favoured paintwork of all royal limousines: dark claret with a scarlet coach line. A doppelganger was built for the Queen's regal visit to Canada that year.

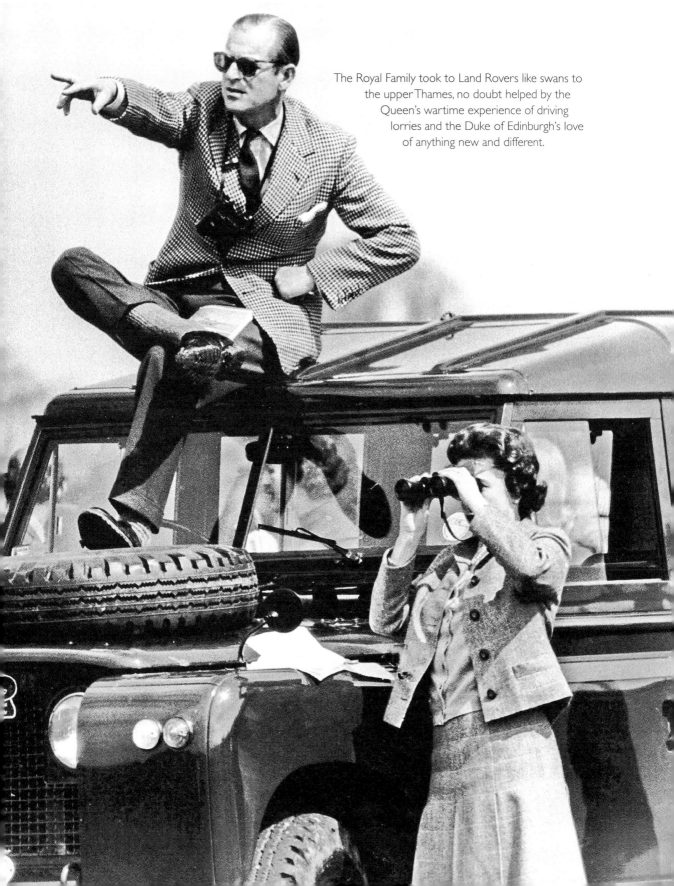

The Royal Family took to Land Rovers like swans to the upper Thames, no doubt helped by the Queen's wartime experience of driving lorries and the Duke of Edinburgh's love of anything new and different.

Scottish engineer James Cuthbertson came up with the idea of fusing a Land Rover's nimbleness with the relentlessly effective use of tracked wheels, as on a tank. He sold them to farmers with undulating, marshy land where reducing ground pressure was a benefit. Using a sturdy subframe, each track used four narrow road wheels, complete with pneumatic tyres, and industrial-strength power steering was, of course, included ...

LAND ROVER

This is thought to be Mr Cuthbertson himself at the wheel, demonstrating the first of some fifteen similar vehicles he built between 1960 and 1972. A few of them were employed to tread delicately in bomb-disposal manoeuvres.

'The World's Most Versatile Vehicle' claim could be in no doubt in this image of Rover's mobile display unit at an open-air trade show, with Eagle refuse collector and Simon 'cherry-picker' Series II conversions arrayed for the perusal of local council fleet buyers.

LAND ROVER

The scene at Salisbury Cattle Market in 1965; throughout rural Britain, the picture would be the same, always with at least one Land Rover in the car park, as farmers drove into town to inspect the livestock, many carting trailer-loads of animals backwards and forwards.

LAND ROVER

Virginia McKenna playing Joy Adamson in the big-screen version of *Born Free* that was released in 1966 to huge acclaim and box-office success. Land Rover continues today to support the charitable Born Free Foundation subsequently established by McKenna and her co-star Bill Travers. Its main aim is to keep wild animals actually in the wild, like Elsa the lioness who melted filmgoers' hearts.

OPPOSITE TOP: George and Joy Adamson and their stories of nurturing lion cubs in Kenya led them to write a best-selling book called *Born Free* (1960), which helped develop a whole new respect for endangered African wildlife.

OPPOSITE BOTTOM: Naturally, the Adamsons had a Land Rover of their own, this well-used Series II with its own travelling compartment for some surprisingly playful big cats.

GRIPPING PHOTOS OF THE 4X4 PIONEER

ABOVE: In the passenger seat of this Series II is secret agent John Drake in a scene from 1960s British TV series *Danger Man*. The character was brought to life by actor Patrick McGoohan, while the palm trees poking up at the back of the set are trying to make the Elstree Studios backlot resemble somewhere dangerous and exotic.

LEFT: The right Land Rover is a guarantee of authentic period atmosphere in any film or TV series, such as here on the Yorkshire set of ITV's 1960s-set police drama series *Heartbeat*, where the village of Goathland doubled for the fictional Aidensfield. It is a short-wheelbase Series IIA.

LAND ROVER

ABOVE: British European Airways is one of the ancestors of BA, and this Vickers Viscount one of its workhorses. It makes a suitably dynamic British backdrop for these two Series IIA station wagons, the like of which could be found working at airports around the world in all kinds of support and emergency roles. From 1968, headlamps were moved out to the wing fronts to meet new lighting rules.

RIGHT: A Land Rover on standby at the airport at Montego Bay, Jamaica, now known as Sangster International Airport after a former Jamaican prime minister, in the late 1960s.

GRIPPING PHOTOS OF THE 4X4 PIONEER

Land Rover offered fire-appliance conversions from very early on, and in Series IIA 109in wheelbase form this FT/6 example was created by outside company Carmichael in 1961. The driver and front passenger seats were shifted to a position ahead of the engine so three more fire crew seats could be squeezed on board, as well as allowing space for a powerful pump, hose reels and rescue equipment.

Conquering rough ground in a Series II 109in wheelbase pick-up.

GRIPPING PHOTOS OF THE 4X4 PIONEER

A Land Rover 109in pick-up demonstrating a remarkable feat of strength by hauling a fleet of its own kind on a freight wagon along railway tracks. You can see the regulation-standard British Rail horns fitted at the front and, of course, the flanged wheels. Rover staged this stunt to mark the IIA's launch in 1961.

LAND ROVER

This dramatic 'worm's eye' shot of a Series II 88in-wheelbase hardtop pushing its way through undergrowth allows a good view of the beefy front leaf springs that were so much a part of the vehicle's 'unburstable' character.

During the Land Rover Series IIA era of the late 1960s, the British Army was a hugely important customer to Rover, buying on average 3,000 military-specification examples every year. Rover worked closely with army chiefs and outside contractors to put some sort of Land Rover into every sphere of defence. The Australian and New Zealand armies were also valued customers. This 109in wheelbase pick-up could pack three-quarters of a ton of squaddies and their kit.

LAND ROVER

A British Army Series IIA 88in short wheelbase stuffed to the gunwales with radio equipment in readiness for battlefield communications.

Indomitable vehicles though they were, Land Rovers were no good to the British Army in one key respect; they couldn't be airlifted into battle by helicopter. They were too heavy. So Land Rover spent three years perfecting a lightweight 'Military Half Ton' that fitted the role for the Fighting Vehicles Research & Development Establishment at Chertsey, Surrey, and it entered service in 1968. For the urgency of battle, they made it work without doors, windscreen, bumpers or rear seats, shedding 500lb in weight. Making the track 4in narrower also helped to get them into the holds of military transport aircraft, from where some were even parachuted into action, using airbags to cushion the blow when they landed.

OPPOSITE: Action Man got his own Land Rover Military Half-Ton in not terribly durable moulded plastic, and this leaflet told all junior commanders exactly how to get it ready for the mother of all battles, until, that is, tea was ready.

LAND ROVER

PALITOY REGD
ACTION man ARMY LANDROVER

The Army Landrover has been specially designed by the ROVER CO. in conjuncton with the British Fighting Vehicles Research and Development Establishment to meet the needs of the British Army & Royal Marines.

It weighs just over one ton, has a 2.25 litre, 4 cylinder engine, and can travel at a maximum speed of 65 m.p.h. over rough terrain.

This versatile and robust vehicle can be dropped by Helicopter, into battle areas and used in many roles, as a command vehicle for infantry and Artillery, personnel carrier, stretcher carrier, or for towing light support weapons.

1

The steering wheel is free moving. (This does not operate the front wheels).

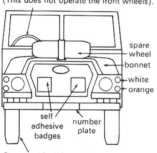

spare wheel
bonnet
white
orange
self adhesive badges
number plate

Care must be taken not to puncture your realistically designed tyres.

The bonnet is hinged and locks in the closed position. A slight amount of pressure may be needed to unlock the bonnet.

palitoy Palitoy Ltd., Coalville, Leicester, England.

2

To unlock the tailboard, first lift clear of the retaining lugs and drop down, reverse procedure to lock.

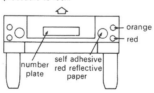

orange
red
number plate
self adhesive red reflective paper

3

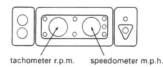

tachometer r.p.m.   speedometer m.p.h.

Position self adhesive speedometer and tachometer stickers as indicated.

4

The spare wheel is held in position by the locating straps which hook into the three raised fittings on the bonnet.

5

The sidelights have a locating pin on the back which fit into a receiving hole on the body.

L III

GRIPPING PHOTOS OF THE 4X4 PIONEER

the world's most versatile vehicle

LAND-ROVER

ABOVE: The cover of the 1962 brochure for the Land Rover Series IIA implied that a strong and manly hand was needed to operate this formidable machine …

RIGHT: Brochure illustration of the Land Rover ladder frame chassis gives a stark idea of how girder-strong the inner vehicle was. The big black box at the centre is the fuel tank.

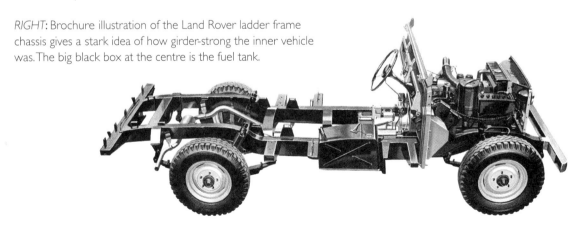

LAND ROVER

The four rear passenger seats in the short-wheelbase 88in station wagon were arranged in face-to-face fashion, hardly the most comfortable arrangement but essential so as to cram in as many passengers as possible.

GRIPPING PHOTOS OF THE 4X4 PIONEER

Land Rover's next bespoke vehicle for the British Army was the 101in wheelbase Forward Control model. The troops needed a four-wheel-drive truck for carrying up to a ton of equipment, and so Land Rover pushed the driving compartment right up to the front to make the load bay bigger, and fitted the powerful all-aluminium V8 engine and transmission from the Range Rover so there was pulling power in abundance. This was ample, in fact, to send drive to the axle of a specially designed, 1.5-ton cargo trailer; the coupling to allow maximum articulation was a masterpiece of precision engineering. It was made from 1972 until 1978.

LAND ROVER

Not many vehicles come with a shovel strapped to the front as standard kit. Then again, the 101 Forward Control was never offered to the public, although enthusiasts rescued and now cherish many ex-army examples that otherwise would have been scrapped. Its place in the UK military fleet was later taken by the four- and six-wheel-drive Steyr-Puch Pinzgauer from Austria.

Here comes Mr Grippy: this Series IIA ice cream van can normally be found plying for trade on the beach in Whitby, North Yorkshire, where it stands little chance of getting bogged down in the sand. Operator Trillo's offers the Whitby Jet, an all-black ice-cream-and-cone combo.

Dormobile built quite a few camper vans using a Land Rover as a basis but would turn its hand to just about anything. This special Series IIA van was built for government officials for forays into the backwoods of Britain to check unscrupulous vendors were not tampering with the quality of the petrol and diesel being sold.

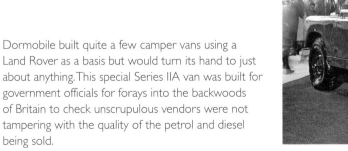

GRIPPING PHOTOS OF THE 4X4 PIONEER

LAND ROVER

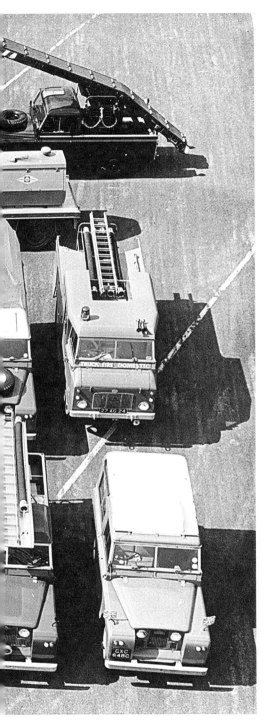

A remarkable factory photo showing the amazing diversity of ways Land Rover Series IIAs could be specified. The mobile cinema (second from top on the left) and circular-saw power take-off (bottom left) contrast cutting room and cutting edge, while the Shorland armoured car version (second row from the top, in the middle) with its rotating turret and Browning .30in gun is perhaps the most awe-inspiring.

Series IIA acting as an aircraft luggage loader; its continuously moving rubber conveyor belt activated by the central power take-off point behind the cab; the whole thing stacks up pretty well.

LAND ROVER

An impressive-looking gooseneck trailer pulled by this Series IIA, with an even more formidable Roadless tractor on the back, circa 1969.

Wintertime feeding for cattle made easy with a Series IIA 109in pick-up, the ideal vehicle for tackling both mud and snow on any farm.

LAND ROVER

All looks a bit dodgy from a health and safety at work viewpoint, but there's no doubt that the Land Rover Series IIA pick-up can handle these guys' attempt to get wood.

GRIPPING PHOTOS OF THE 4X4 PIONEER

Excellent summertime reading in 1972 with this special issue of *Tiger*. The comic's in-house racing driver hero, Skid Solo, is leading the charge in an off-road adventure, and although the grille badge is indistinct, there's no doubting he's at the wheel of a trick Land Rover Series IIA!

LAND ROVER

Life imitating art: designers at Aardman Animation created a none-too-faithful short-wheelbase Land Rover for their hit 2007 TV series *Shaun the Sheep*, and then Land Rover built a replica in real life, using bits and pieces from a variety of old models to get the fantasy look just right, to the delight of kids everywhere.

This 1972 Harrier Air Drive backhoe loader turned the Series III Land Rover into a stand-in JCB, its stabilising feet at the back making sure the vehicle didn't topple over if it hit a buried boulder. It has to be about as far from the luxury SUVs Land Rover makes today as it is possible to get.

The majority of Land Rover-based ambulances have always been destined for military or United Nations use, but a few others have been built to work in territories around the world where four-wheel drive was essential to get to the emergency. This Series III, for instance, was made by caravan firm Rollalong and destined to see service in Nigeria.

ABOVE: Be afraid, be very afraid, especially if you were considering a coup in a far-off country in the early 1980s. One of these in the hands of the authorities, legitimate or otherwise, would be likely to put down any dissent. It is SMC Engineering's Sandringham 6 Hotspur armoured patrol car. The extra pair of driven wheels gave 50 per cent more grip and braking and, vitally, doubled the payload, which meant it could cope with light armour plating *and* a ten-man crew with half a ton of equipment in the air-conditioned interior. The V8-powered vehicle could issue warnings with its searchlight and PA system but could then actively attack a building with its barricade ram, gas dischargers, and gun ports. It could then retreat on run flat tyres. Almost as scary as a rabid dictator himself …

RIGHT: One of the images issued by Land Rover in 1973 to promote the then-current Series III 109in station wagon to the buying public; no raked gravel and pretty sunsets here, just sheer, roaring, mud-scattering, brute-force action!

GRIPPING PHOTOS OF THE 4X4 PIONEER

Hiding in the long grass is the one-millionth Land Rover, a Series III 88in station wagon. It was painted in a unique metallic green colour and given a black velour interior, and it did a big tour of dealers to spread the news of this important milestone. The first 250,000 had been built by November 1959, the 500,000th by April 1966 and the 750,000th by June 1971.

Land Rovers made great breakdown trucks, even at a tabletop size like this Corgi Juniors toy in appropriately garish 1970s purple.

LAND ROVER

This impressive fleet of Series III 88in hardtops is shown in 1976 when they were brand new and being handed over to the British Coastguard service for deployment all around the country's shores.

Versatile power take-off points were a much-valued Land Rover feature from the very beginning. The motive energy is here coming off the front take-off point to activate a pulley on a piece of machinery, with special metal chocks under the front wheels to hold the Series III vehicle steady for its task of work.

LAND ROVER

The AA's Land Rovers still had a lot of towing to do in the early 1980s. Here one of its ever-patient patrolmen is explaining the unpowered steering technique to the anxious owner of a Ford Fiesta whose car has conked out in, of course, a ford. The 88in van is one of the last Series IIIs built in 1983.

Deep in the forest in 1977 with a colour co-ordinated Series III 88in station wagon.

LAND ROVER

ABOVE: Land Rover customers continually asked for vehicles that could handle even more hard work, and in 1982 the company introduced this super-tough high-capacity pick-up on the 109in wheelbase. It boosted carrying capacity to 1.3 ton and came with suspension suitably beefed up to cope, plus a guard rail to stop any heavyweight cargo slamming into the back of the cab in an emergency stop.

OPPOSITE TOP: Land Rovers were adopted by almost every police force in Britain for their ability to cope and intervene in every imaginable emergency or condition. This Series III 109in station wagon belonged to London's Metropolitan force in 1979.

OPPOSITE BOTTOM: Workmen are here still putting the finishing touches in 1980 to the Humber Bridge linking Yorkshire and Lincolnshire. The Land Rover Series III patrol vehicles, though, are all ready for their working lives ahead, rescuing drivers from the fog, rain and wind that plagues the estuary, and looking out for suicidal leapers thinking of plunging into the murky water.

LAND ROVER

ABOVE AND OPPOSITE: Launched in 1979, the V8 version of the Series III finally put some real fire in the Land Rover's belly to give it extra muscle off-road and much better performance on tarmac. The engine came straight from the very successful Range Rover, and in fact so did the LT95 four-speed transmission, which meant this was the first Series III to have permanent four-wheel drive just like its luxury cousin. Engineers had to rein back its eagerness, though, because the Land Rover brakes couldn't handle the Range Rover's 132 brake horsepower; it became 91 bhp for the Land Rover, but it still felt like a Ferrari in comparison to all previous Landies.

GRIPPING PHOTOS OF THE 4X4 PIONEER

LAND ROVER

A few touches of sparing comfort and style were added to factory-built Land Rovers for the first time in April 1982. The County station wagons had arrived, in smart two-tone paintwork and with redesigned, cloth-upholstered seats. Those for the driver and outer passenger even had headrests. There was tinted glass and even a bit of soundproofing material in the headlining to cut the booming racket when driving long distances on-road. It was the very earliest evidence that the rough-and-ready Land Rover was starting to be tamed and civilised for mass consumption.

In 1983 the Series III was declared dead as the traditional Land Rover range underwent its most radical technical transformation in thirty-five years. In came the heavily revised 110 and with it a Range Rover-style chassis where the unforgiving leaf springs were replaced by heavy-duty coil springs in the suspension system, as shown in this 'ghosted' graphic. It had to happen, really: Land Rover's dominance of the four-wheel-drive market was under multiple attack from Japanese rivals ranging from the Mitsubishi Shogun to the Toyota Hilux pick-up, and most of them were a jolly sight less jarring in everyday use than a Land Rover.

The Land Rover 90 was the new short-wheelbase model and was now also offered with the V8 engine and all of its extra urge, which was much appreciated by Britain's equestrian community.

A left-hand-drive Land Rover 110 with scissor-lift platform for working at height, and four stabilising legs to keep it steady.

Land Rover continued to be the go-to manufacturer for light military vehicles, but forces were naturally wary of the new coil-spring suspension. Was it up to the job? Here test drivers from the Australian Army put a 110 pick-up through its paces to find out in 1985. They must have been impressed because, after a few modifications had been ordered, some 2,500 were requested, with a side order of 400 6x6 models, a contract worth A$150 million.

LAND ROVER

The consumer-market accessories list for the 90 and 110 models burgeoned in the 1980s, helping buyers customise their Land Rovers in the he-man off-roader vogue that spread from the USA. This one has a full-length roof rack, a winch, huge extra spotlamps, and a front bull bar, that latter feature soon to cause controversy in the UK as concerns for pedestrian safety mounted.

A lovely bit of dry stone walling here, along with one of two special 90s built to celebrate Land Rover's fortieth anniversary in 1988 and finished in appropriately traditional tones.

This decidedly racy 90 soft top was a one-off called the Cariba. It was unveiled in 1987 as an indication of how Land Rovers might be adaptable into fun cars rather like Suzuki's pint-sized four-wheel-drive SJ. The leather seats from a Range Rover, metallic paint, styled wheels and padded rollbar certainly looked good, but the high cost of the basic vehicle meant it couldn't have competed with budget-priced Japanese upstarts.

A handsome and smartly turned out 90 station wagon of the late 1980s, now boasting a new turbodiesel engine but demonstrating how timeless the basic Land Rover remained.

In 1988 Land Rover embarked on a five-year sponsorship of Cowes Week, the annual sailing festival off the Isle of Wight, and there was no better way to signal this than by joining in. So this amphibious 90 took to the waters, its buoyancy aids drawing on years of British Army experience with similar waterborne Land Rovers.

New for 1984 was a dramatically extended chassis option with a 127in wheelbase, but this one-off stretched monster built in 1991 was claimed, at 22ft in total, to be the very longest Land Rover in the world. It was specially made by Special Vehicle Operations at the Solihull factory for Eastern Electricity (now UK Power Networks), and stationed at its Ipswich headquarters. V8 power and six-wheel drive meant it could get anywhere quickly to fix a broken power cable.

GRIPPING PHOTOS OF THE 4X4 PIONEER

Land Rover won an order for 800 of these Defender XD 130 battlefield ambulances for the British Army in 1996, but not before the basic vehicles had undergone punishing evaluation tests, and been strengthened internally. The bodies – of the vehicles, not the casualties – came from Marshall of Cambridge.

A Defender 110 station wagon, fitted with Monroe shock absorbers, doing what few so-called off-road vehicles are capable of – genuine rock-hopping.

OPPOSITE TOP: Adventurer and explorer Sir Ranulph Fiennes had this military-specification Defender 110 XD specially adapted so he could attempt something no one had ever done before: to drive right around the world in a 21,000-mile band from the west coast of Ireland, across Europe, through Russia and over the Bering Straits. From there he intended to cover the whole of Canada until he reached the Newfoundland coast, and then it would be back to Ireland. The demountable tracks were just one part of the vehicle. Another was a power take-off that meant it could drive on to a special pontoon whose propeller the Land Rover could then bring to life and steer from its driving seat. It was such a shame that Sir Ranulph's sponsor dropped out and the planned 1997 Global Expedition never happened, but there is no reason why someone couldn't give the trip a go now.

OPPOSITE BOTTOM: In one of the biggest movie car fleets of all time, Land Rover built thirty-one of these twenty-second-century urban vehicles for the big-screen outing ofcomic-strip hero Judge Dredd, and delivered them to Pinewood Studios in 1994. Only this one was fully trimmed and operable (they used second-hand 101in army chassis, picked for their height), the others all being hollow shells used as props to represent taxis in a forbidding and futuristic Mega-City 01.

LAND ROVER

GRIPPING PHOTOS OF THE 4X4 PIONEER

From 1990 the traditional Land Rovers adopted the model name of Defender to mark them out from the new Discovery sport-utility vehicle and the Freelander compact off-roader being designed in secret. The 90 and 110 appellations were kept for short- and long-wheelbase models, while the extra-length 127 was renamed the 130 to make it sound snappy, although three extra inches were not, in fact, added to its wheelbase. So, here we have the box-fresh Defender 130 turned out as a pick-up with four-door crew cab – a highly desirable mix of the Defender's vast array of elements.

Special brew: six-wheel adaptations of Land Rovers have long been part of the marque's wondrous 'biodiversity', sometimes built at the Solihull factory and sometimes by outside engineers.

LAND ROVER

Curiously, Land Rovers had never been very successful in the USA, but in the 1990s there was a renewed push to interest North American buyers in this quintessentially British 'truck', with a V8-powered 110 station wagon and an open-topped 90 specially tailored to the local market. Here's the 90 in Land Rover's 1995 line-up that, naturally enough, was dominated by the opulent Discovery and Range Rover. Ever-tightening legislation that demanded airbags (the Defender had none) expelled it from the USA after 1997.

One of the most distinctive facets of Land Rovers and Range Rovers has been their body panels made from aluminium, for lightness and resistance to corrosion. Here are raw aluminium bodies waiting to be turned into production-line vehicles at Solihull in the mid-1990s, a Defender following a second-generation Range Rover on the left, with a Discovery in the foreground.

GRIPPING PHOTOS OF THE 4X4 PIONEER

Land Rover Defenders are essential to emergency services everywhere, not just in the UK but in places like Italy, where the local police have run scores of them like this.

The Italian fire service is rife with Defenders too; they all carry special 'VF' number plates that signify Vigili Del Fuoco, for fire-fighters, and presumably ensures instant exemption from speed cameras …

ABOVE AND OVERLEAF: Aspects of Defender in the twenty-first century: the off-road tenacity remains undimmed, but the Meccano-like riveted construction, exposed components, ruler-straight lines and tiny old-fashioned lights are wonderfully out of step with the organic look that has pervaded all exterior automotive design in the new millennium.

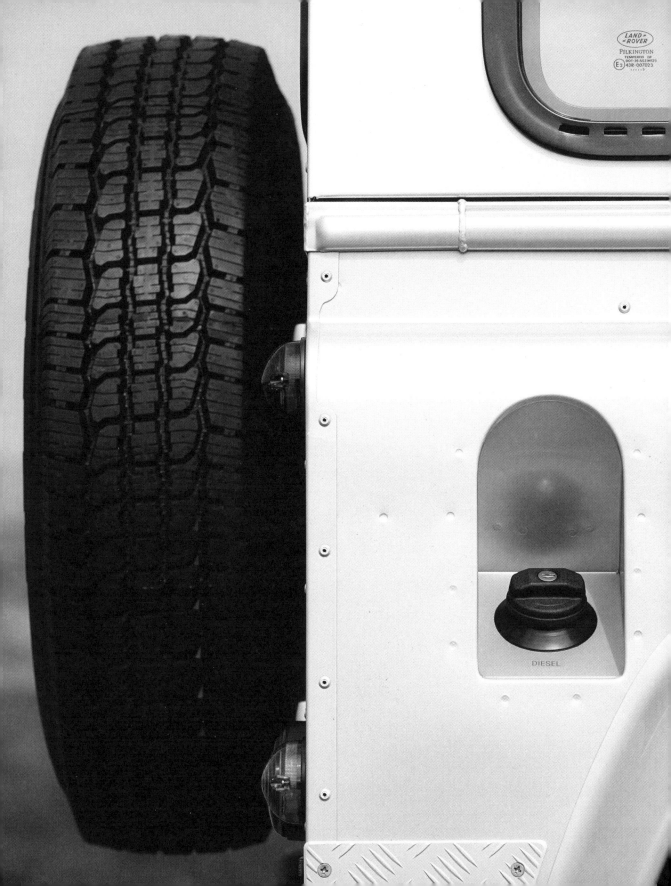

Land Rover Defender 130 pick-up, lots of logs, mud, country air, presumably a big appetite developing for supper.
Who wants to work in an office, eh?

LAND ROVER

GRIPPING PHOTOS OF THE 4X4 PIONEER

Land Rover Defenders are not meant to be racing cars, which is probably obvious from their brick-like shape and towering stature. But the fine-tuning of experts at Bowler Motorsport in Derbyshire could give one an awe-inspiring ability to cover rough ground in double-quick time. From 2014 to 2016, Land Rover supported a rally series exclusively for these Bowler-modified machines. The crowds may have been sparse but the competitors loved the hair-raising action, challenging each other in identical cars fitted with 170bhp 2.2-litre diesel engines, six-speed manual gearboxes and a fully approved motor-sport roll cage. Each one cost £50,000.

OPPOSITE: The two-millionth Defender – that is, 2 million of all the traditional Land Rovers – was signed by everyone who built it and completed its unique specification. This included survival expert Bear Grylls. Bonhams sold it for £400,000, which made it the most expensive Land Rover ever, and the proceeds were split between Land Rover's three favoured charities: the International Federation of Red Cross, Red Crescent Societies and the Born Free Foundation.

LAND ROVER

Fishermen certainly won't approve if you use your
Defender for shortcuts along rivers, but at least
you know you're all set for any flash flood that our
increasingly volatile climate throws at you.

Land Rover's very own 'Jungle Track' beside the manufacturing plant at Solihull, plus some wild countryside on the Eastnor Castle estate in Herefordshire, have themselves become hallowed Land Rover ground. For newcomers to the phenomenal off-road capability of the Defender, plus other less austere members of the marque portfolio, they are challenging enough to conquer any fears about taking on water, mud, unforgiving gullies and frightening-looking inclines. With, of course, civilisation just a stone's throw away.

LAND ROVER

GRIPPING PHOTOS OF THE 4X4 PIONEER

You tend to most readily associate Aston Martins and Lotuses with spectacular on-screen sequences in James Bond movies, but in 2012 the Land Rover Defender broke their stranglehold on 007 action. This 110 Double Cab was raced against a train in the opening sequence of *Skyfall* by the Secret Service's field agent Eve Moneypenny. Naomie Harris, or someone who looks at a distance the dead spit of her in a Belstaff jacket, was at the wheel.

The Defender 110 Double Cab from Bond epic *Skyfall*, cleaned up and glitteringly presented to the world in the window of Harrods department store in London's Knightsbridge in October 2012 – fifty years to the very week that 007 first appeared at the movies.

Revelling in its new-found exposure to Bondmania, the Defender was back in the 2015 movie *Spectre*, changing sides this time as Spectre's ruthless assassin Mr Hinx and his henchmen gave chase in Defender double cabs. They were heavily modified with enormous 37in tyres and super-resilient suspension by Land Rover's Special Vehicle Operations, as was an accompanying Range Rover Sport SVR. These images were taken on set during filming on the Gaislachkogl mountain at Sölden in the Austria Alps. Three years later the 007 Elements experience opened at the same snowy spot 3,050m above sea level; the Hoffler Klinik in the film is actually the ice Q restaurant, and the trick Defender was there for fans to marvel at.

GRIPPING PHOTOS OF THE 4X4 PIONEER

It is 2009 and the British Red Cross Defender 110 station wagon is here seen stepping into action to help householders deluged by the devastating floods in Cockermouth, Cumbria.

More British Red Cross volunteers helping out whenever a little light snow brings the UK to a grinding halt. Proficiency behind the wheel of a Defender ambulance is a skill almost as valuable as CPR …

The five-seater 110 utility wagon, an estate car and van in one, was actually a new variant in the Defender range of 2009. By then the whole range had undergone a raft of improvements to keep it compliant with new car build rules. These included new engines, the first ergonomically designed dashboard, and a quieter six-speed transmission.

Being kind to its environment, rather than squaring up to it, was something quite new to the Defender. Land Rover engineers nonetheless built an experimental pure-electric 110 pick-up in 2013, and found the perfect venue to test it out in the real world: Cornwall's eco-friendly Eden Project. It could haul this 12-ton road train of carriages laden with sixty visitors and create zero pollution in the process, with its Hill Descent Control-linked braking system generating battery power as it whirred silently downhill. It could toil a low-speed, eight-hour day on one overnight charge, which cost just £2.

GRIPPING PHOTOS OF THE 4X4 PIONEER

You can buy a different four-wheel-drive car to a Defender to patrol the outer reaches of your rural retreat. But why would you?

OPPOSITE TOP: The world-famous Beaulieu Autojumble is a giant, twice-yearly flea market for old car parts in the fields surrounding Lord Montagu's country seat in Hampshire. Such is the clamour for original parts that the obsolete products of Solihull have their own dedicated section at the spring fixture, aptly entitled the 'Land Rover Rummage'.

OPPOSITE BOTTOM: Trailers, pallets, spanners, frowning and elbow grease – the essentials of rebuilding classic Land Rovers.

LAND ROVER

GRIPPING PHOTOS OF THE 4X4 PIONEER

The Land Rover Defender 90 station wagon as visualised by Sir Paul Smith in 2015. The twenty-seven exterior colours were all carefully chosen by the legend of British fashion. 'I wanted deep rich colours, but at the same time I wanted them to work together yet be surprising,' he said. 'The Defender is a British icon, which is something I'm exceptionally proud of. I keep a Defender at my home in Italy, which is in the middle of the countryside.'

LAND ROVER

GRIPPING PHOTOS OF THE 4X4 PIONEER

Well into the twenty-first century, Defenders were still being built the traditional way – mostly by hand, by time-honoured assembly workers steeped in Land Rover's traditions of choice and versatility.

GRIPPING PHOTOS OF THE 4X4 PIONEER

LAND ROVER

Here it is, the very last 'proper' Land Rover, sent on its way amid thunderous applause from 700 past and present staff who know it like the faces of their children. 'The Defender is a special vehicle and very much hand built,' said one, David Smith, who worked on the line for thirty-seven years. 'You need to get a feel for it; we call it "the knack" and it takes months to learn the knack.' Now David had to develop a new knack, building the Jaguar XE at the same plant.

OPPOSITE PAGE: These are moments from the day, 29 January 2016, that every Land Rover aficionado dreaded: the very last day of production for the Defender and, so, the final breath of life for a direct lineage stretching back sixty-eight years. By then, it took fifty-six hours to complete one, using 7,000 parts including the external door hinges that workers called 'pigs' ears'. Amazingly, there were still two components fully interchangeable between the 1948 Series I and the 2016 Defender: the hood cleats and an underbody support strut.

GRIPPING PHOTOS OF THE 4X4 PIONEER

Twenty-five Land Rovers, some of them shown here, performed a solemn 'funeral procession' at the Solihull factory on 16 January 2016 to say goodbye to a British motoring legend even more venerable than the Mini. In all, 2,016,933 closely related Series Is, IIs, IIIs, 90s/110s and Defenders were made.

LAND ROVER

The Defender's distinctive 'clamshell' bonnet that sits proud of its box-like contours is one of the vehicle's few metal bits with any curvature to it. The slats, grilles and open screw heads like these have all been smoothed away on modern cars by the imagination of designers and the demands of the showroom, but the Land Rover character relayed through its right-angled contours remains undimmed.

ABOVE AND OPPOSITE: Land Rover sprung a surprise in 2018 by announcing it would create a limited edition of 150 'Works V8' models. It wasn't the much-loved vehicle returning to production, sadly, but a nifty makeover of existing Defender 90 station wagons. The centrepiece of the car was a 5-litre V8 engine crackling with 400bhp of power, which not only made it the most powerful Defender ever but also provided an incredible, Porsche-crushing 0–60mph acceleration time of 5.6sec. Top speed, strictly limited by the shed-like aerodynamics, was 106mph. An eight-speed ZF automatic gearbox was also installed, along with fancy alloy wheels, a choice of eight colours, machined aluminium accessories and LED headlights. The Recaro seats and full re-trim in gorgeous black leather was a sight to behold, as well it should be at a hefty £150,000.

LAND ROVER

A Defender Heritage limited edition, casually at home while rock climbing.

LAND ROVER

Old Land Rovers rarely die – they just find new places to go and new stuff to do. This Series I known as 'The Landy' had reached the end of its long road in 2015 when its four joint owners, friends from university, decided it was beyond repair and reluctantly put it up for auction after fifteen fun-filled years. The wife of one of them, though, had other ideas, and with Land Rover's help secretly bought the car and had it brought back to rude health, using mostly genuine parts. It meant that flabbergasted co-owners Will Radford, Jeremy Wells, Anthony Dawson and James Shatwell were presented with it on 14 February 2015. Here it is on the shingle foreshore of the Ahuriri Valley on New Zealand's dramatic South Island.

LAND ROVER

An all-new Defender? Can it really be done and the credibility of the original be preserved? Fans are waiting to find out in 2020 but Land Rover seems bent on hitting new heights of off-road capability. Here one of the hard-worked prototypes lands in Kenya for some punishing shakedown testing.

LAND ROVER

Scorching hot tarmac or freezing cold snow, any new Defender will have to be dependable enough to cope with both. Prototypes of the 2020 heir to a legend have been all round the world in the engineers' quest to break them.

The all-new Defender is setting out to conquer new heights, taking the spirit of Solihull, Maurice Wilks and British ingenuity along with it.